Welcome, dear adventurer, to a world reimagined in shades of gray, where your creativity holds the key to unlocking its vibrant essence. This coloring book is your invitation to embark on a journey of self-discovery, relaxation, and artistic expression.

Within these pages lie images waiting to be infused with the colors of your imagination. Each stroke of your pencil, brush, or crayon will bring them to life, revealing hidden depths and unlocking their potential for beauty. Whether you seek peaceful tranquility, creative inspiration, or a mindful escape from the everyday, this book holds the promise of a transformative experience.

No artistic expertise is required. The simple act of coloring offers a therapeutic pathway to de-stress, unwind, and reconnect with your inner child. As you lose yourself in the mesmerizing process of applying color, your worries will melt away, replaced by a sense of calm and serenity.

This book is your personal canvas, a blank slate upon which you can paint your own unique vision. Embrace the freedom to experiment, explore different color palettes, and let your creativity flow freely. There are no rules, no expectations, just the joy of creating something beautiful and uniquely yours.

As you color, pay attention to the emotions that arise within you. Allow the colors to become your language, expressing what words cannot. Each shade you choose can tell a story, reveal your inner world, and connect you to your deepest emotions.

This book is more than just a coloring book; it's a portal to a world of self-discovery, mindfulness, and creative expression. So, grab your favorite tools, find a comfortable space, and let your imagination lead the way. Welcome to the grayscale world, where your creativity is the only limit!

Tony Williams

Metatron,

The angelic scribe and recorder of all creation, stands as a celestial bridge between the divine and the earthly realms. Radiating ancient wisdom and knowledge, Metatron holds the key to unlocking the secrets of the universe. With his fiery scroll and quill of light, he records the events of time and assists humanity in its spiritual evolution.

Prayer:

Oh, mighty Metatron, celestial scribe and keeper of divine secrets, I call upon your wisdom and guidance. Open my mind to the knowledge of the universe and illuminate the path of my spiritual journey. Help me to understand my role in creation and utilize my talents for the benefit of all beings.
Amen.

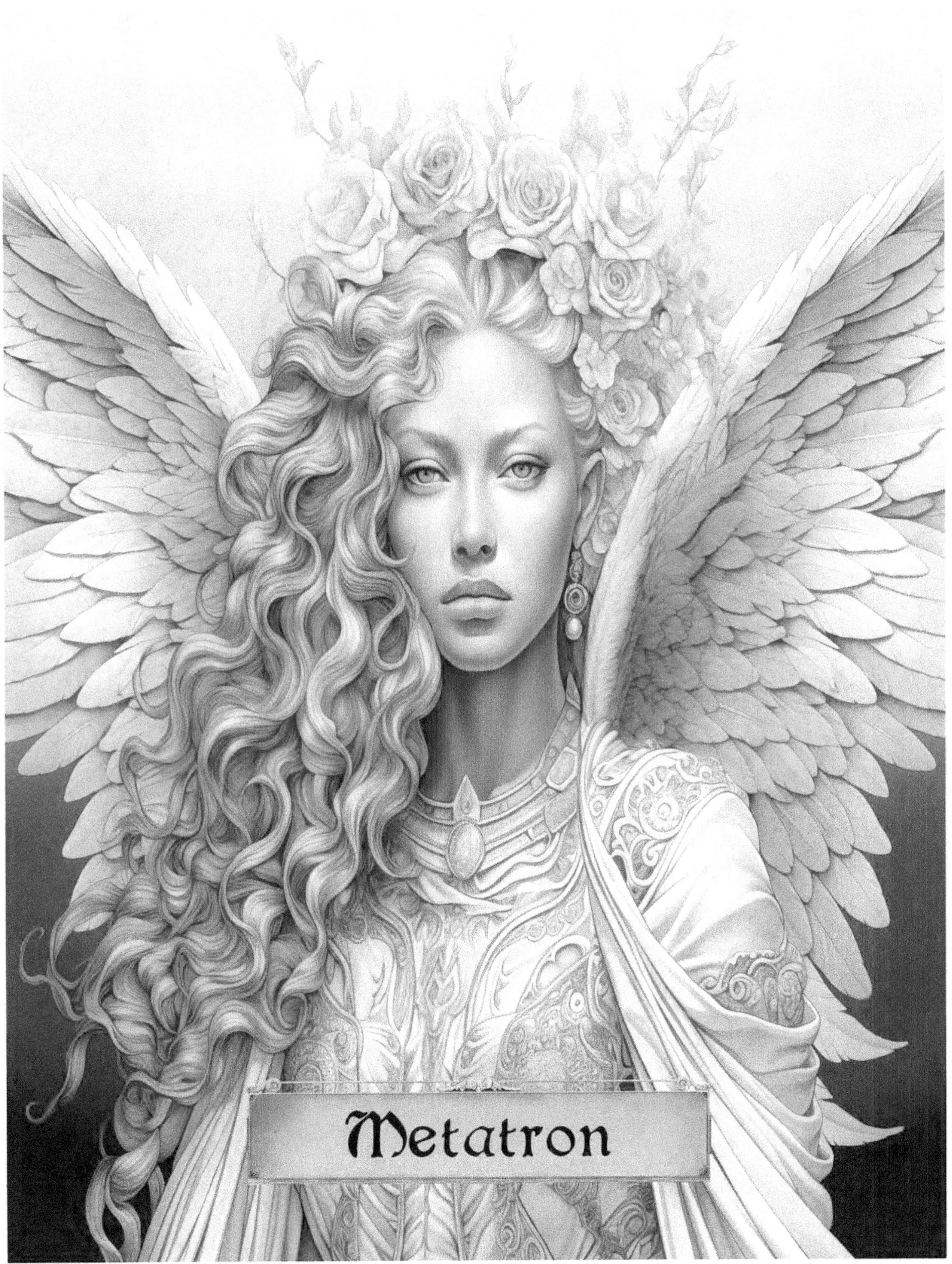

Metatron

Michael,

The valiant protector and champion of justice,
stands as a defender against negativity and darkness.
With his blazing sword and shining armor,
he embodies courage, strength, and unwavering faith.
Michael guides and protects humanity, leading the
way towards righteousness and victory over evil.

Prayer:

Oh, glorious Michael, defender of the faith and
champion of justice, I call upon your strength and
courage. Protect me from all harm and negativity,
and grant me the strength to overcome adversity.
Guide me in my battles against darkness and inspire
me to always stand for what is right.
Amen.

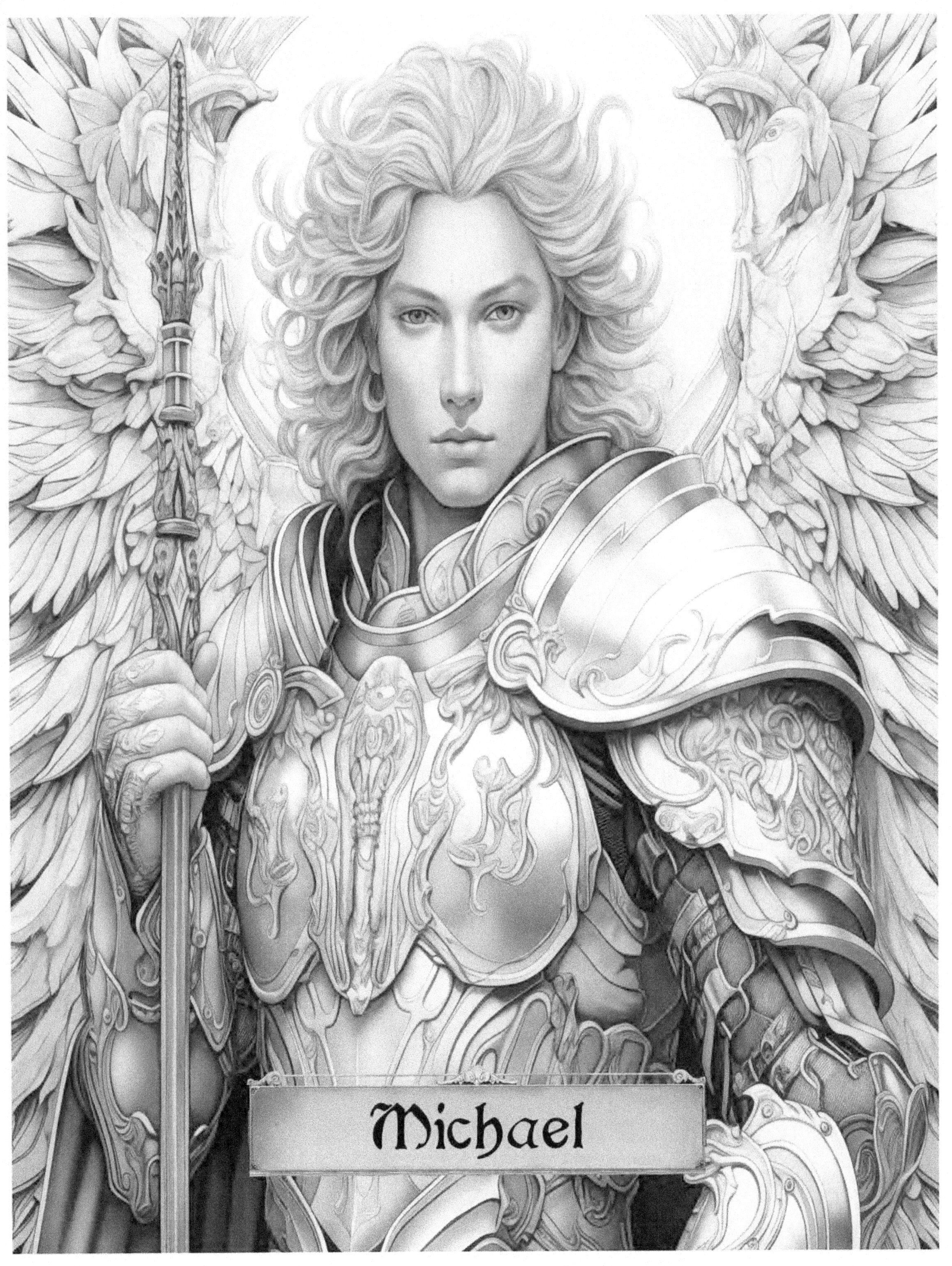
Michael

Gabriel,

The divine messenger and harbinger of hope,
brings forth tidings of joy and new beginnings.
With her gentle presence and silver wings,
she embodies purity, love, and peace.
Gabriel delivers divine messages, inspires creativity,
and provides comfort and support to those in need.

Prayer:

Oh, radiant Gabriel, messenger of hope and
divine love, I call upon your gentle spirit and blessings.
Fill my heart with joy and hope, and guide me
towards new beginnings. Open my mind to receive
divine messages and inspire me to express
my creativity for the good of all.
Amen.

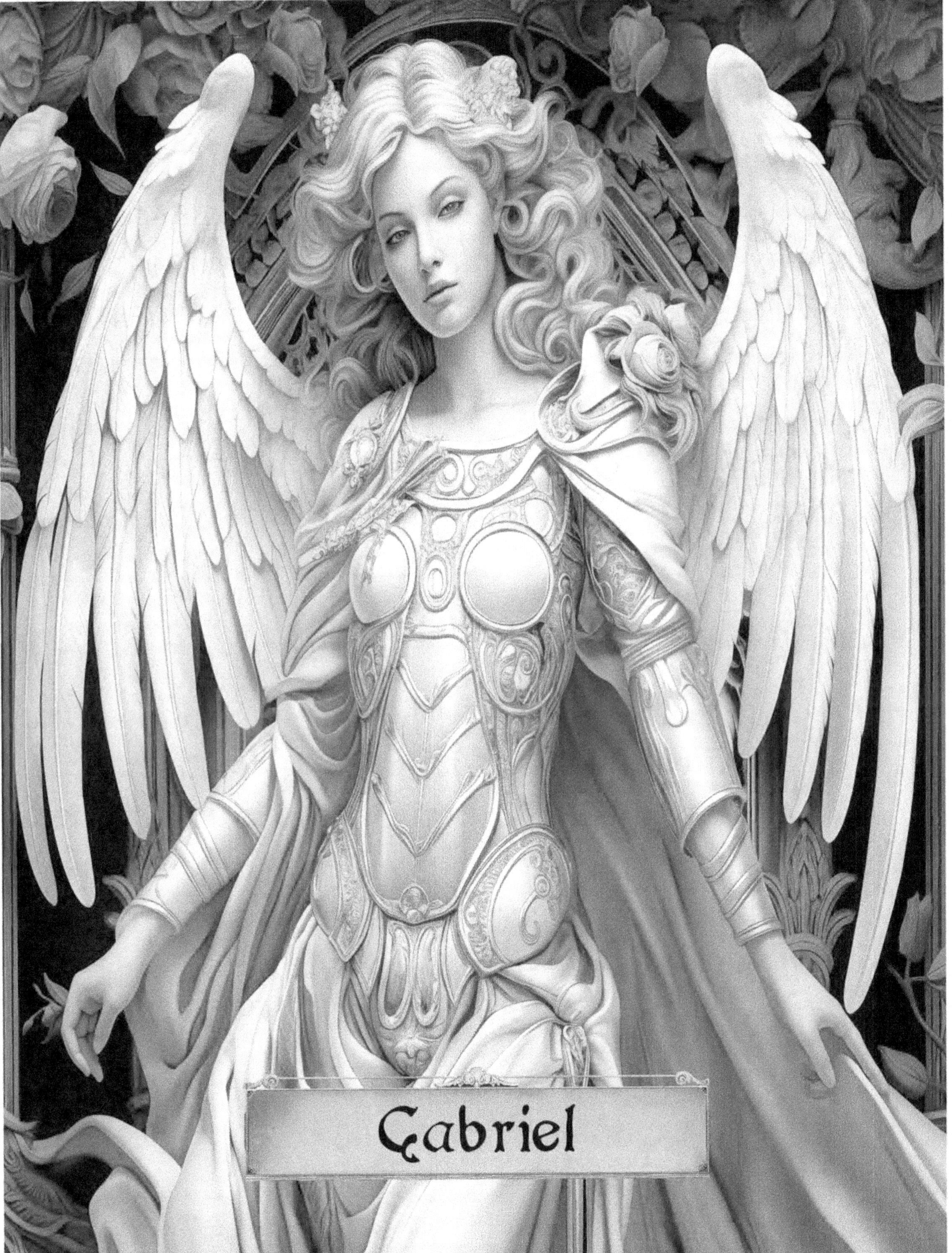
Gabriel

Zadkiel,

The angel of mercy and forgiveness,
embodies compassion, understanding, and healing.
With his soft lavender wings and gentle demeanor,
he offers solace to the afflicted and assists in the process
of emotional and spiritual healing.
Zadkiel promotes forgiveness, reconciliation, and helps
us release past hurts and move forward with peace.

Prayer:

Oh, merciful Zadkiel, angel of forgiveness and healing,
I call upon your compassion and understanding.
Grant me the strength to forgive myself and others,
and heal the wounds of my past. Guide me towards
emotional and spiritual wholeness, and help me
to release negativity and embrace peace.
Amen.

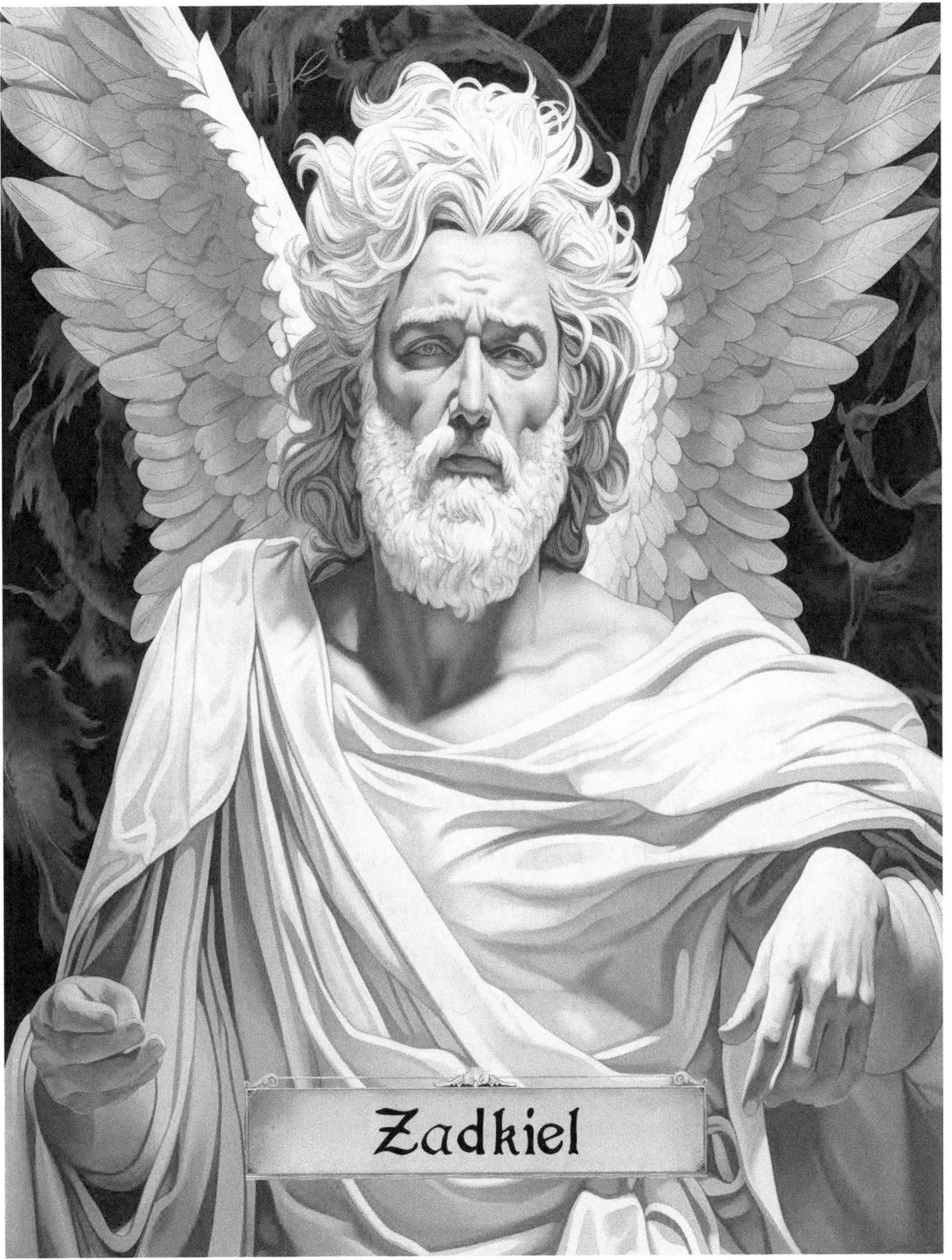
Zadkiel

Camael,

The angel of justice and fairness, upholds divine law and order. With his fiery red wings and unwavering determination, he represents righteousness, strength, and the unwavering pursuit of justice.
Camael protects the innocent, fights against injustice, and ensures that all are treated with fairness and equity.

Prayer:

Oh, righteous Camael, angel of justice and fairness, I call upon your unwavering spirit and strength. Guide me in my pursuit of justice and help me to stand up for what is right. Protect the innocent from harm and ensure that fairness prevails in all situations.
Amen.

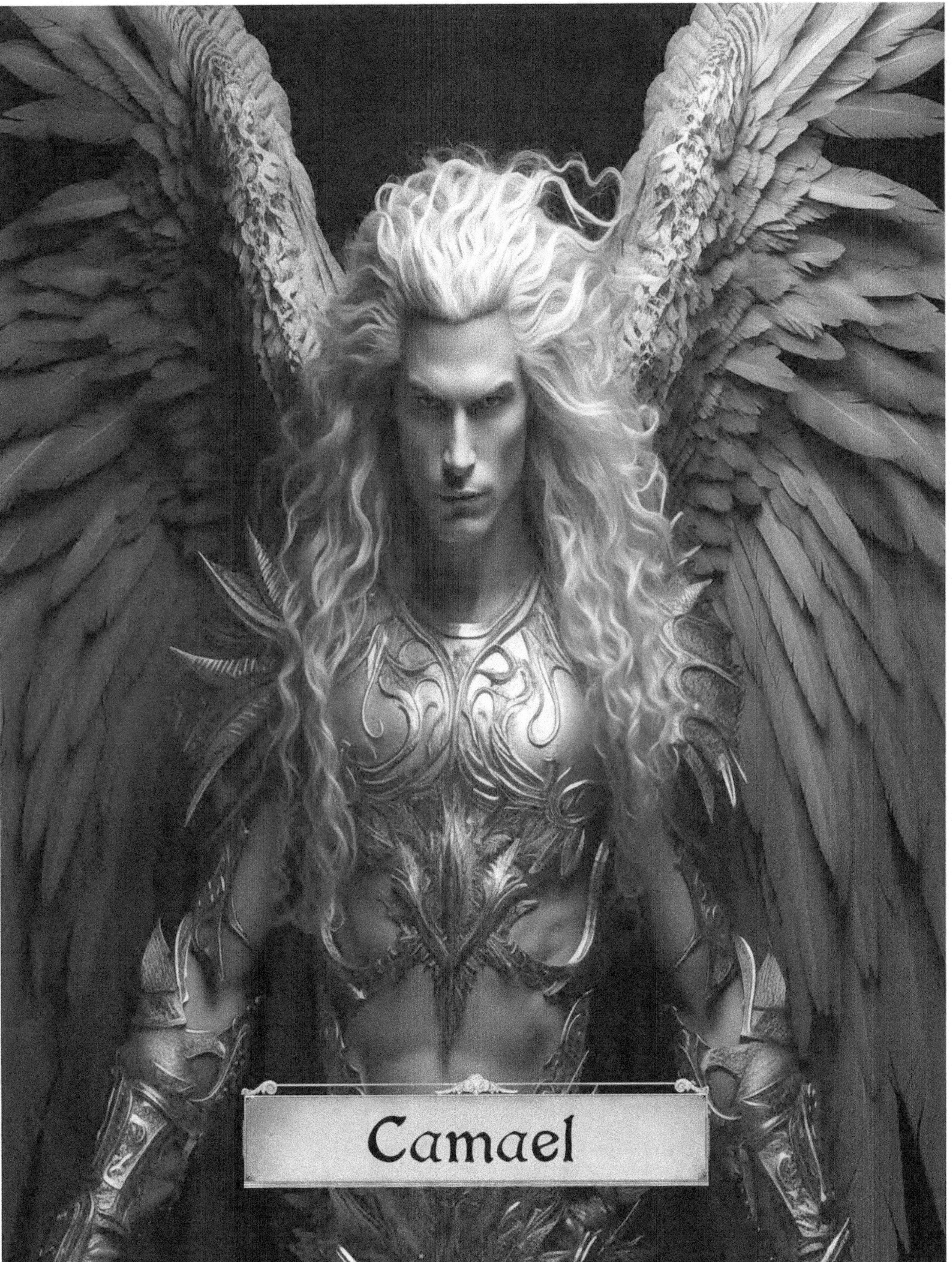
Camael

Haniel,

The angel of joy and abundance,
radiates happiness, creativity, and love.
With her vibrant wings and joyful spirit,
she inspires happiness, gratitude, and the
manifestation of our desires. Haniel encourages
creative expression, fosters love and joy in our lives,
and helps us attract abundance and prosperity.

Prayer:

Oh, joyful Haniel, angel of abundance and creativity,
I call upon your radiant spirit and blessings.
Fill my heart with joy and gratitude, and open
my mind to receive the blessings of abundance.
Inspire my creativity and guide me towards
expressing myself authentically.
Amen.

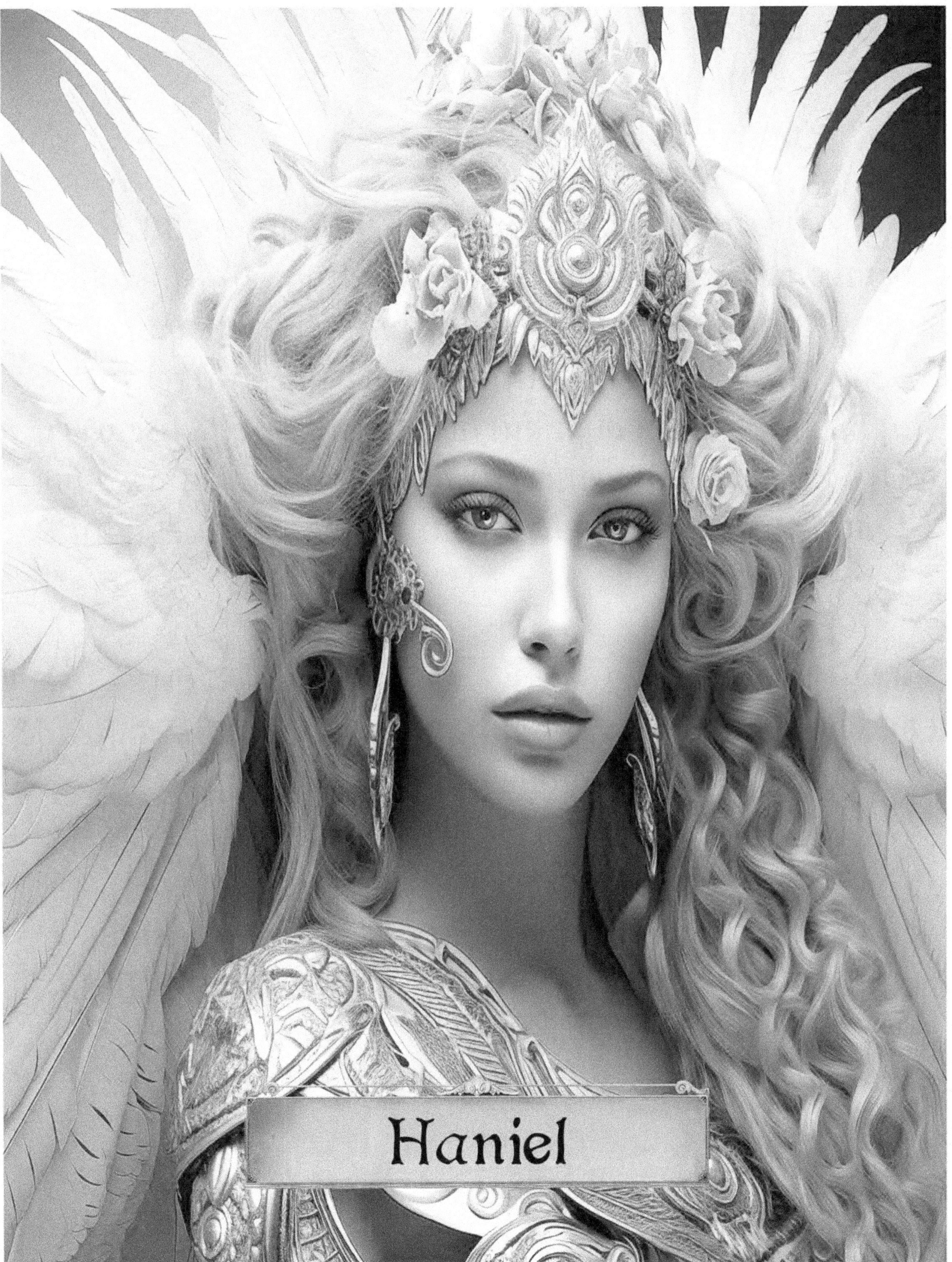
Haniel

Uriel,

The angel of wisdom and enlightenment,
embodies knowledge, understanding, and insight.
With his golden wings and piercing eyes,
he illuminates the path to spiritual awakening
and guides us on our journey towards self-discovery.
Uriel dispels ignorance, awakens our inner wisdom,
and inspires us to live with purpose and clarity.

Prayer:

Oh, wise Uriel, angel of enlightenment and knowledge,
I call upon your wisdom and guidance.
Illuminate my mind with understanding
and help me to see things with clarity.
Grant me the wisdom to make sound decisions
and guide me on my path to spiritual awakening.
Amen.

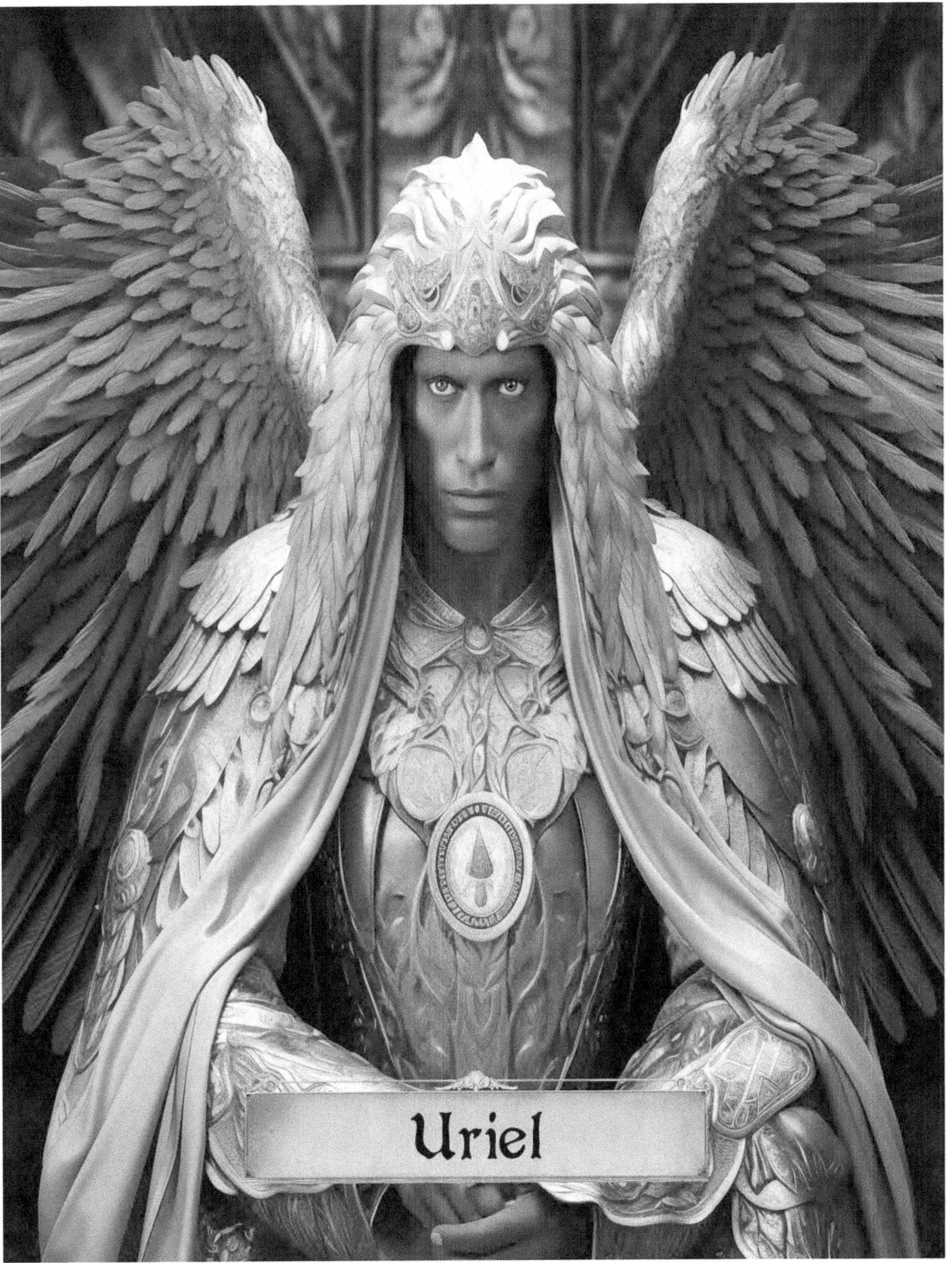
Uriel

Jophiel,

The radiant angel of beauty and inspiration,
embodies creativity, artistic expression,
and inner peace. With her vibrant wings shimmering
in hues of gold and rose, and a playful spirit that
dances on the air, she inspires us to see the beauty
in all things and encourages us to express our
unique talents and gifts. Jophiel brings joy and
light to our lives, reminding us of the inherent
beauty that surrounds us and within us.

Prayer:

Oh, radiant Jophiel, angel of beauty and inspiration,
I call upon your light and creative spirit.
Fill my heart with joy and open my eyes
to the beauty that surrounds me. Guide my hand
and inspire my mind to express my unique talents
and bring joy to the world. Awaken my inner artist
and help me create beauty in all that I do.
Amen.

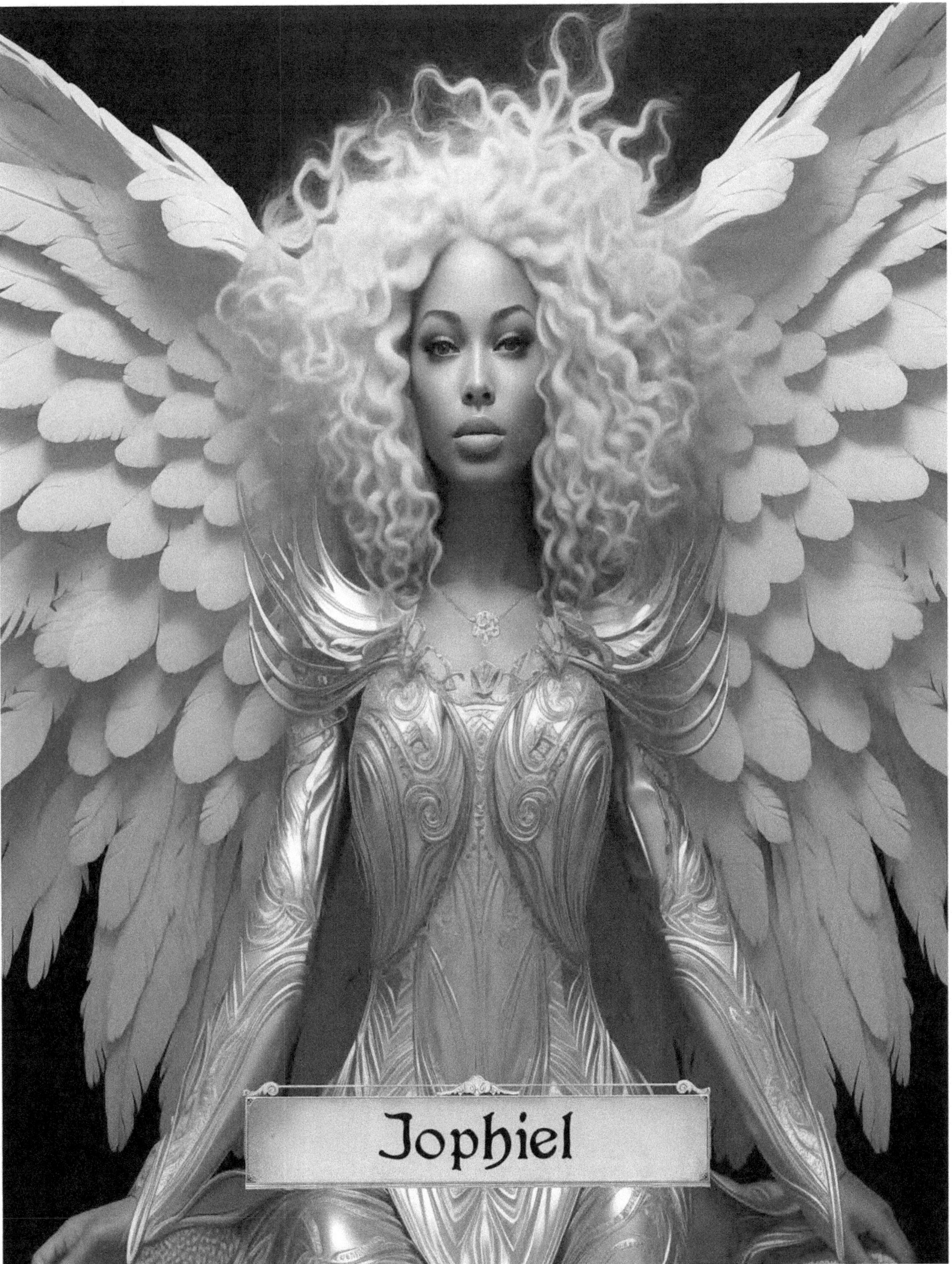

Jophiel

Sandalphon,

The angel of music and Earth connection,
represents grounding, balance, and harmony.
With his earthy wings and gentle demeanor,
he guides us in connecting with the natural world
and promotes inner peace and stability.
Sandalphon helps us manifest our desires on the
Earthly plane and fosters a sense of belonging
and connection to all living beings.

Prayer:

Oh, grounded Sandalphon, angel of music and Earth
connection, I call upon your calming presence
and blessings. Help me find peace and stability
within myself and connect with the Earth's natural
rhythms. Guide me in manifesting my desires
on the physical plane and foster a sense of belonging
and harmony in my life.
Amen.

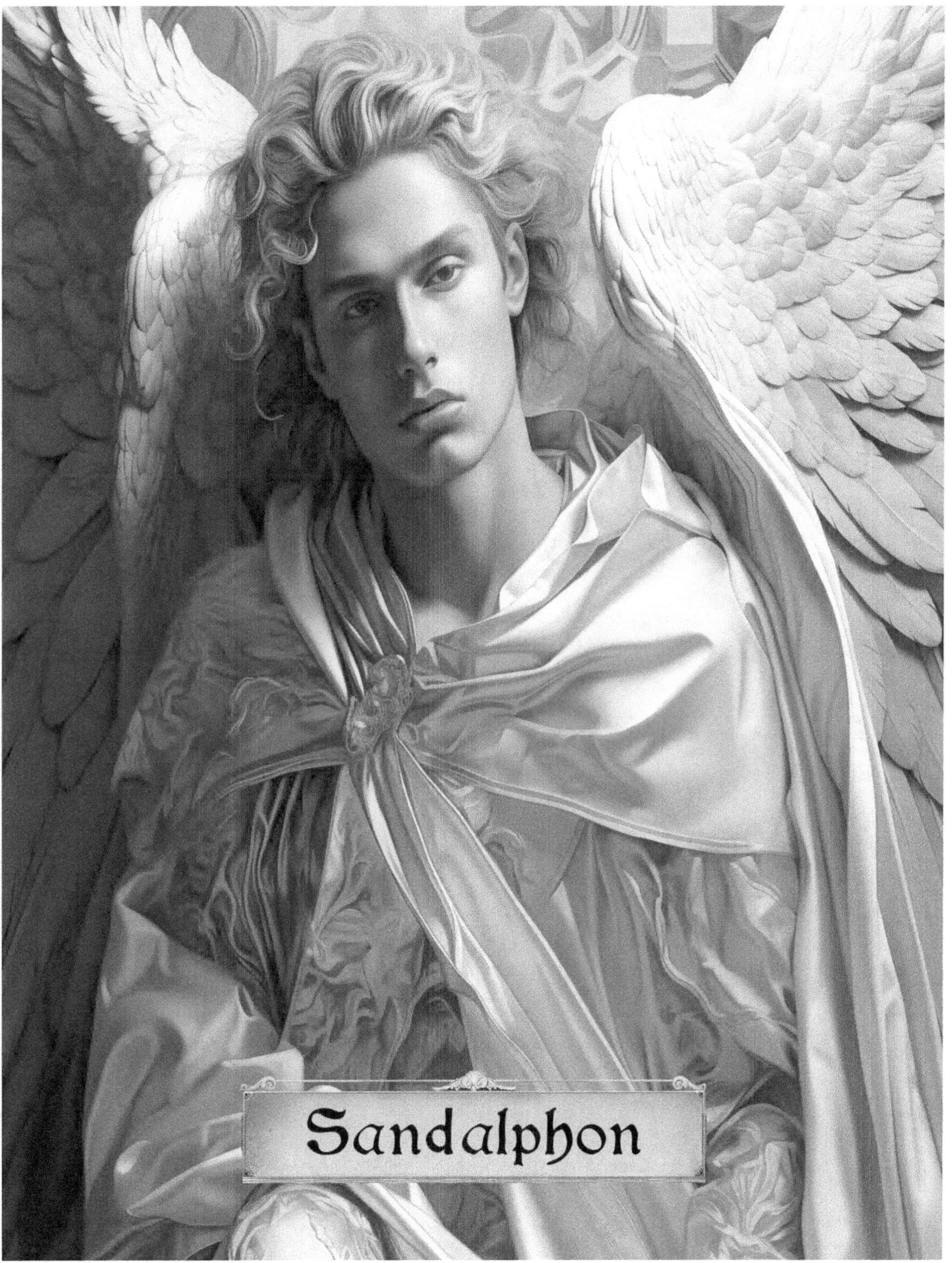
Sandalphon

Raziel,

The angel of knowledge and secrets, embodies
ancient wisdom and hidden knowledge.
With his veiled face and swirling wings resembling
galaxies, he guards the mysteries of creation and
transformation. Raziel offers insights into the past,
present, and future, and guides us on our journey
of self-discovery and spiritual evolution.

Prayer:

Oh, enigmatic Raziel, angel of knowledge and secrets,
I call upon your wisdom and guidance.
Open my mind to hidden knowledge and
illuminate the path of my spiritual evolution.
Help me understand the mysteries of the universe
and unlock the secrets within myself.
Amen.

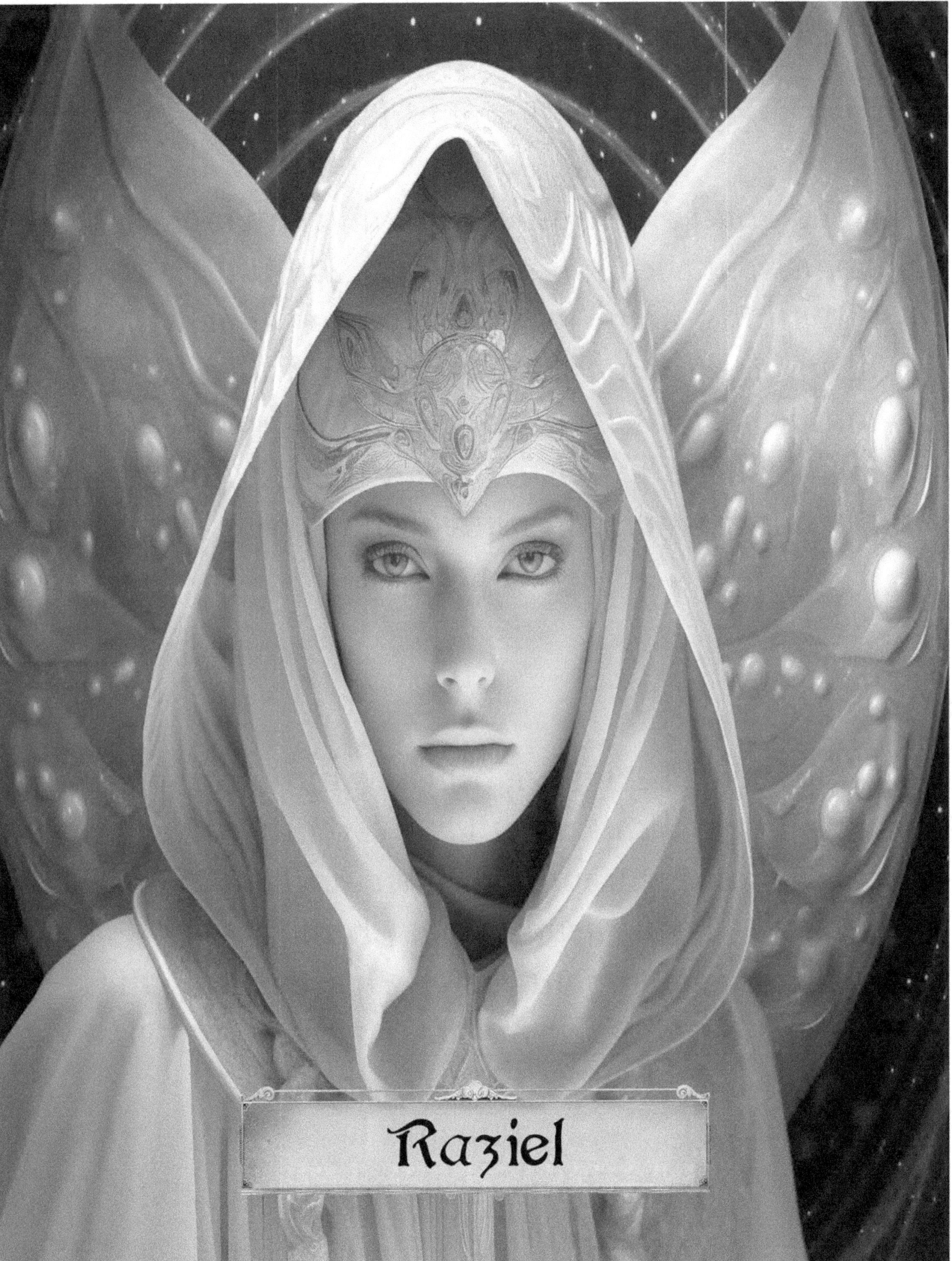

Raziel

Tzaphkiel,

The angel of introspection and contemplation,
embodies patience, self-reflection, and understanding.
With his serene presence and soft blue wings,
he guides us on a journey of inward exploration
and promotes self-discovery and personal growth.
Tzaphkiel helps us release negativity, forgive ourselves
and others, and find peace and acceptance within
ourselves.

Prayer:

Oh, patient Tzaphkiel, angel of introspection and
contemplation, I call upon your serenity and guidance.
Help me quiet my mind and turn inward to explore
the depths of my being.
Lead me on a journey of self-discovery and
orgiveness, and grant me the wisdom to understand
myself more fully.
Amen.

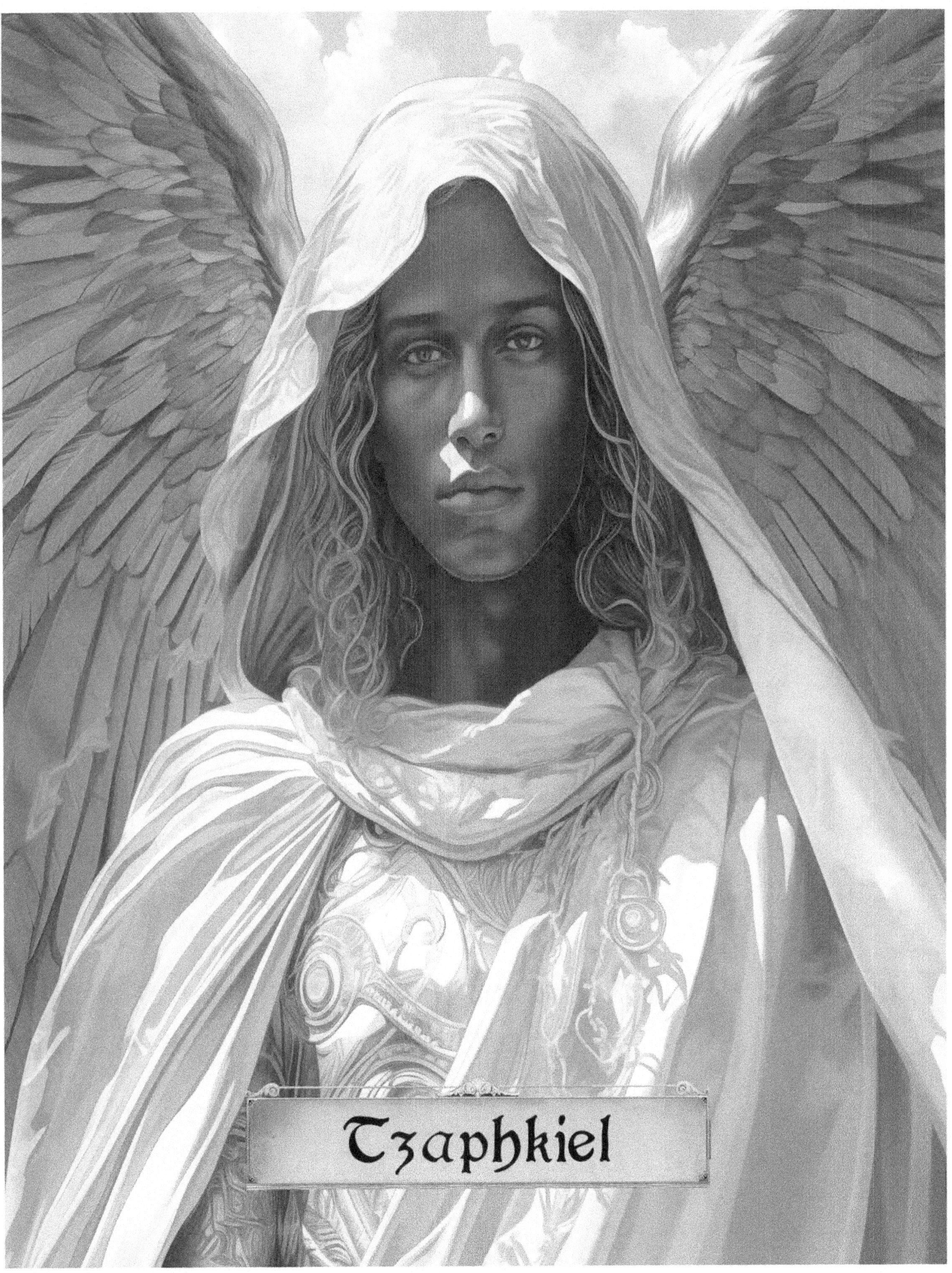
Tzaphkiel

Raphael,

The angel of healing and rejuvenation,
embodies compassion, empathy, and the power of
nature's healing energy. With his emerald green wings
and gentle touch, he brings comfort and restoration
to those in need. Raphael promotes physical and e
motional healing, guides us towards wholeness,
and helps us connect with the healing power
of the Earth.

Prayer:

Oh, compassionate Raphael, angel of healing
and rejuvenation, I call upon your gentle touch
and blessings. Heal the wounds of my body, mind,
and spirit, and guide me towards wholeness
and well-being. Grant me the strength to overcome
illness and inspire me to cultivate inner peace.
Amen.

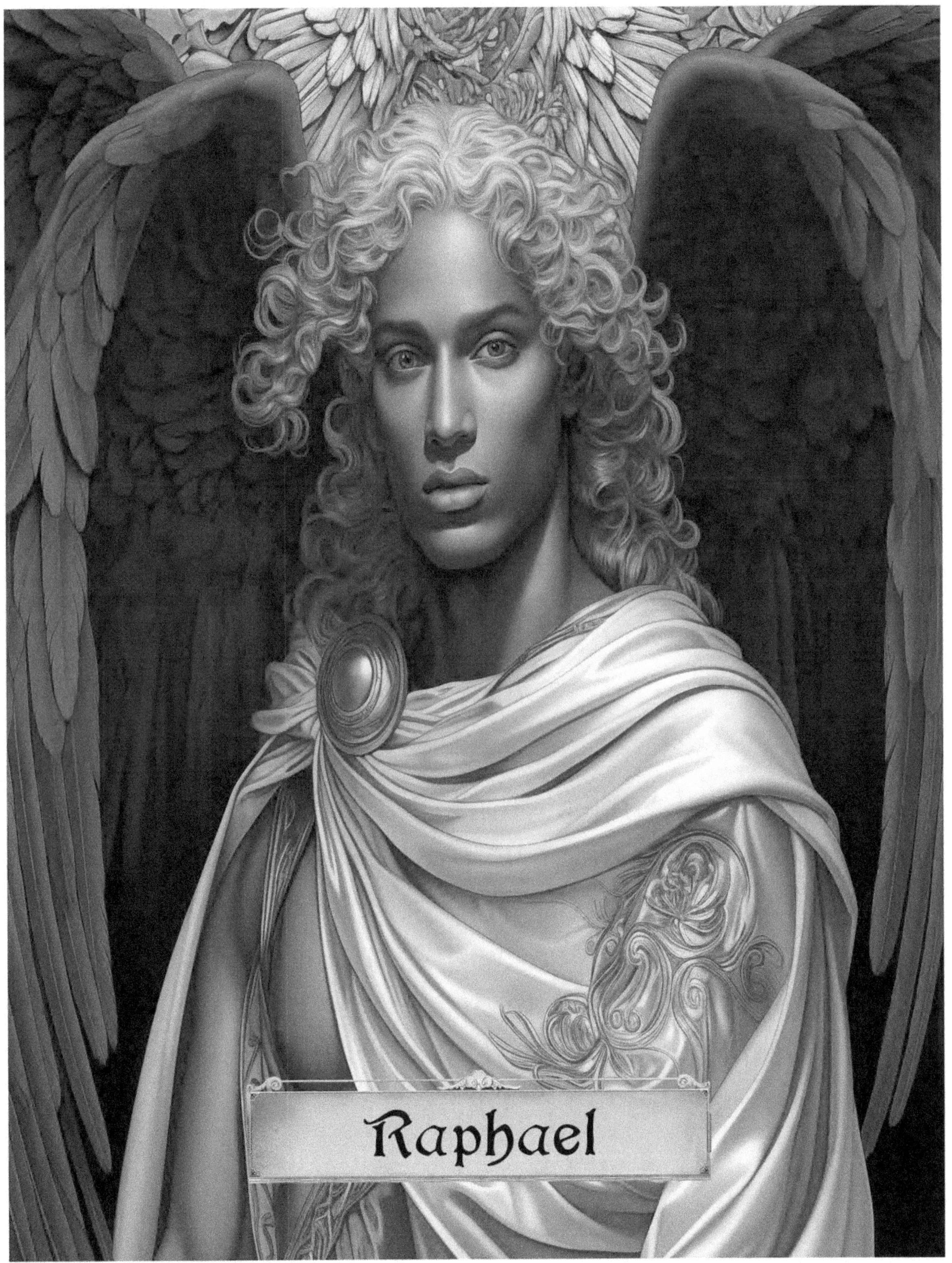
Raphael

Sariel,

The angel of transformation and judgment,
embodies change, redemption, and the
unveiling of truth. With his fiery wings and piercing
eyes, he represents a necessary reckoning and the
potential for rebirth and renewal.
Sariel guides us through transformative periods,
assists us in facing our shadow selves, and helps
us release old patterns and embrace
new beginnings.

Prayer:

Oh, powerful Sariel, angel of transformation and
judgment, I call upon your guidance and strength.
Help me navigate through periods of change and
overcome challenges with courage and grace.
Grant me the wisdom to discern truth from illusion
and guide me towards my highest purpose.
Amen.

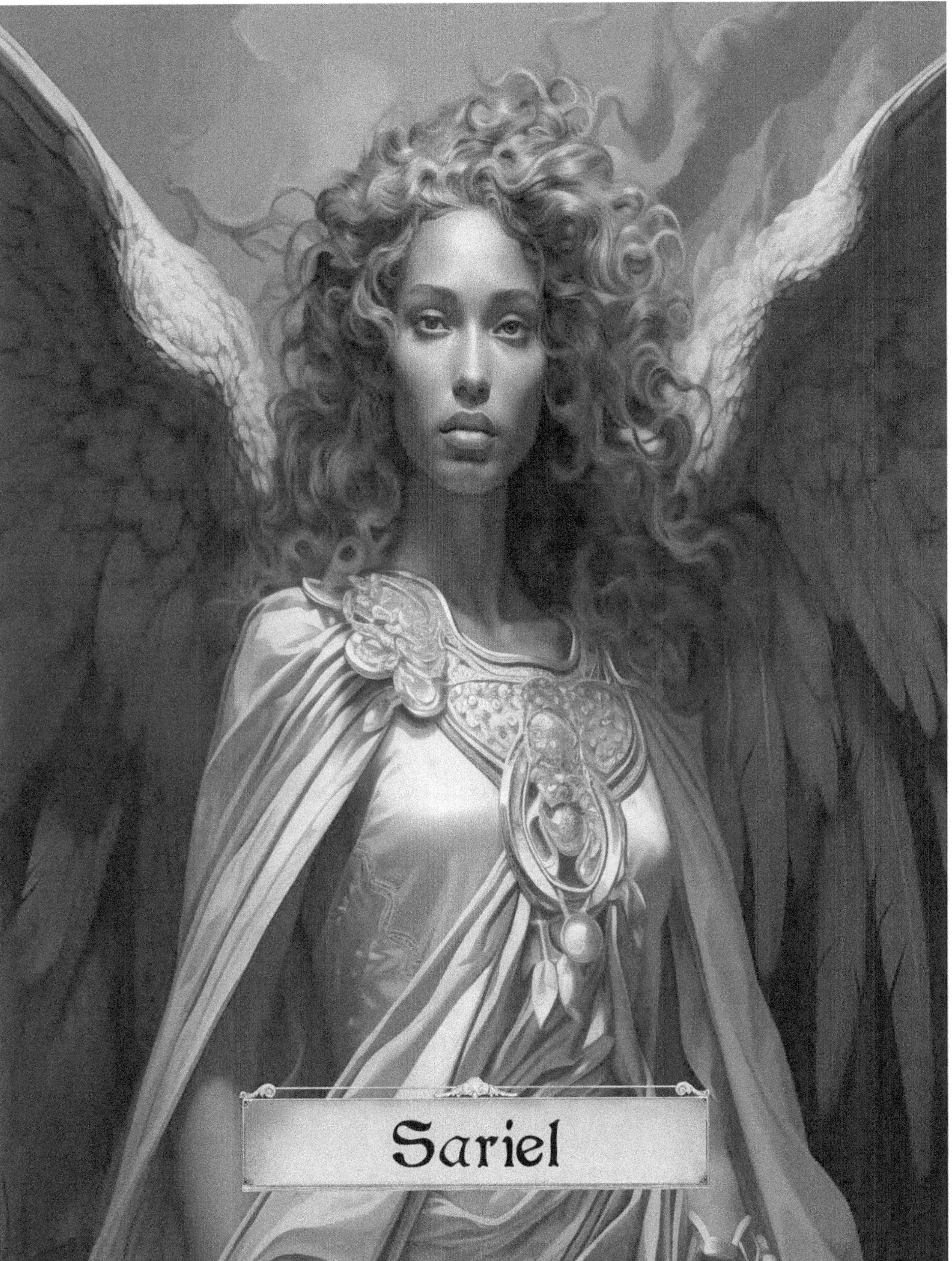
Sariel

Raguel,

The angel of harmony and justice, embodies fairness,
impartiality, and the restoration of balance.
With his white wings and unwavering gaze,
he represents divine law and order and ensures that
justice prevails. Raguel promotes peace and
reconciliation, resolves conflicts, and guides us
towards harmonious relationships with ourselves
and others.

Prayer:

Oh, righteous Raguel, angel of harmony and justice,
I call upon your wisdom and discernment.
Guide me in resolving conflicts and promoting fairness
in all my interactions. Help me to see things from
different perspectives and act with compassion and
understanding.
Amen.

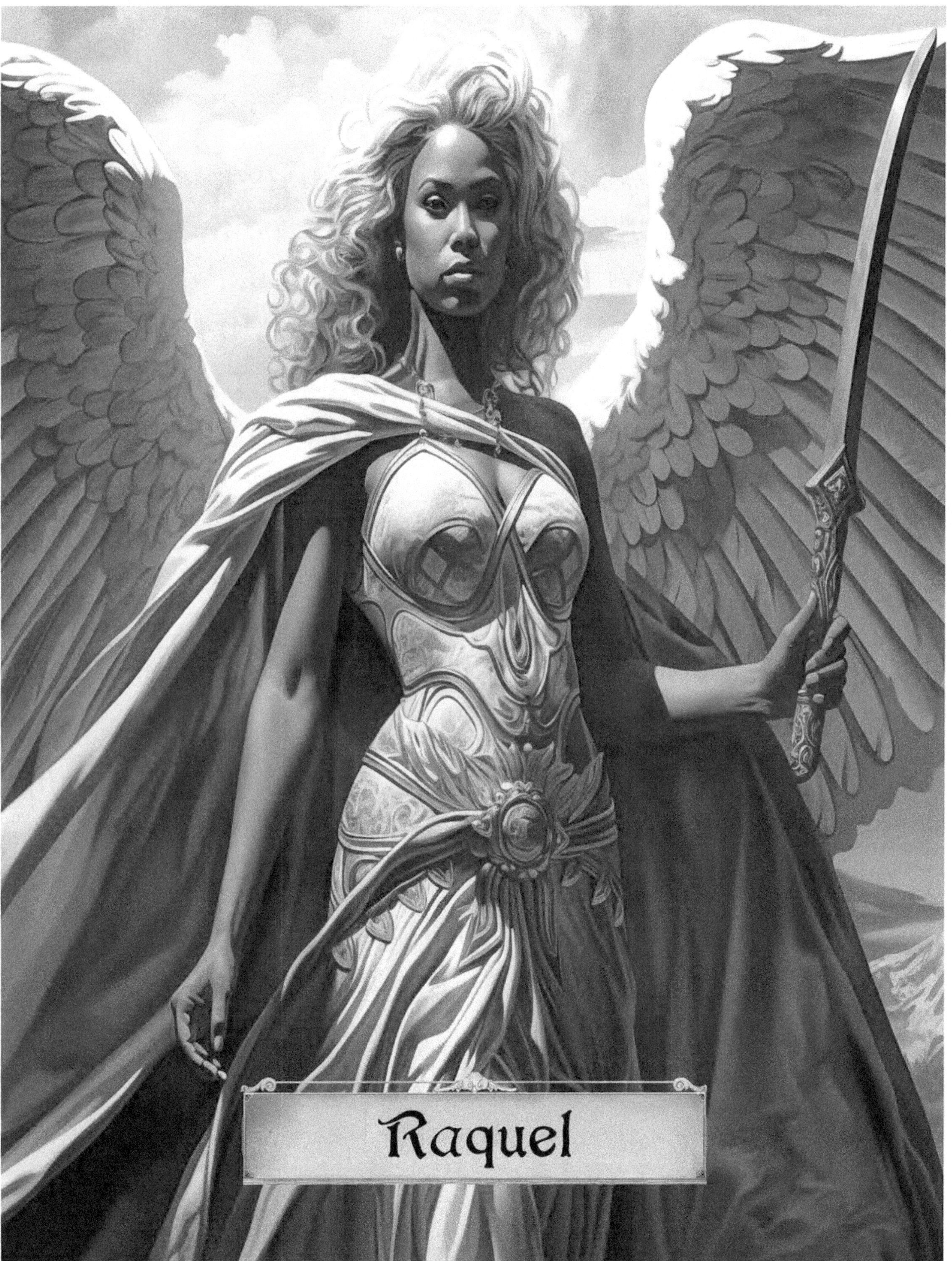

Raquel

Remiel,

The angel of hope and compassion,
embodies forgiveness, mercy, and the power of second
chances. With her gentle demeanor and
soft pink wings, she offers comfort and solace
to those in need and encourages us to extend
compassion and love to ourselves and others.
Remiel helps us forgive our past mistakes,
move forward with hope,
and cultivate inner peace.

Prayer:

Oh, merciful Remiel, angel of hope and compassion,
I call upon your gentle spirit and blessings.
Grant me the strength to forgive myself and others
and move forward with hope and optimism.
Guide me on my journey towards self-acceptance
and compassion, and inspire me to extend
love to all beings.
Amen.

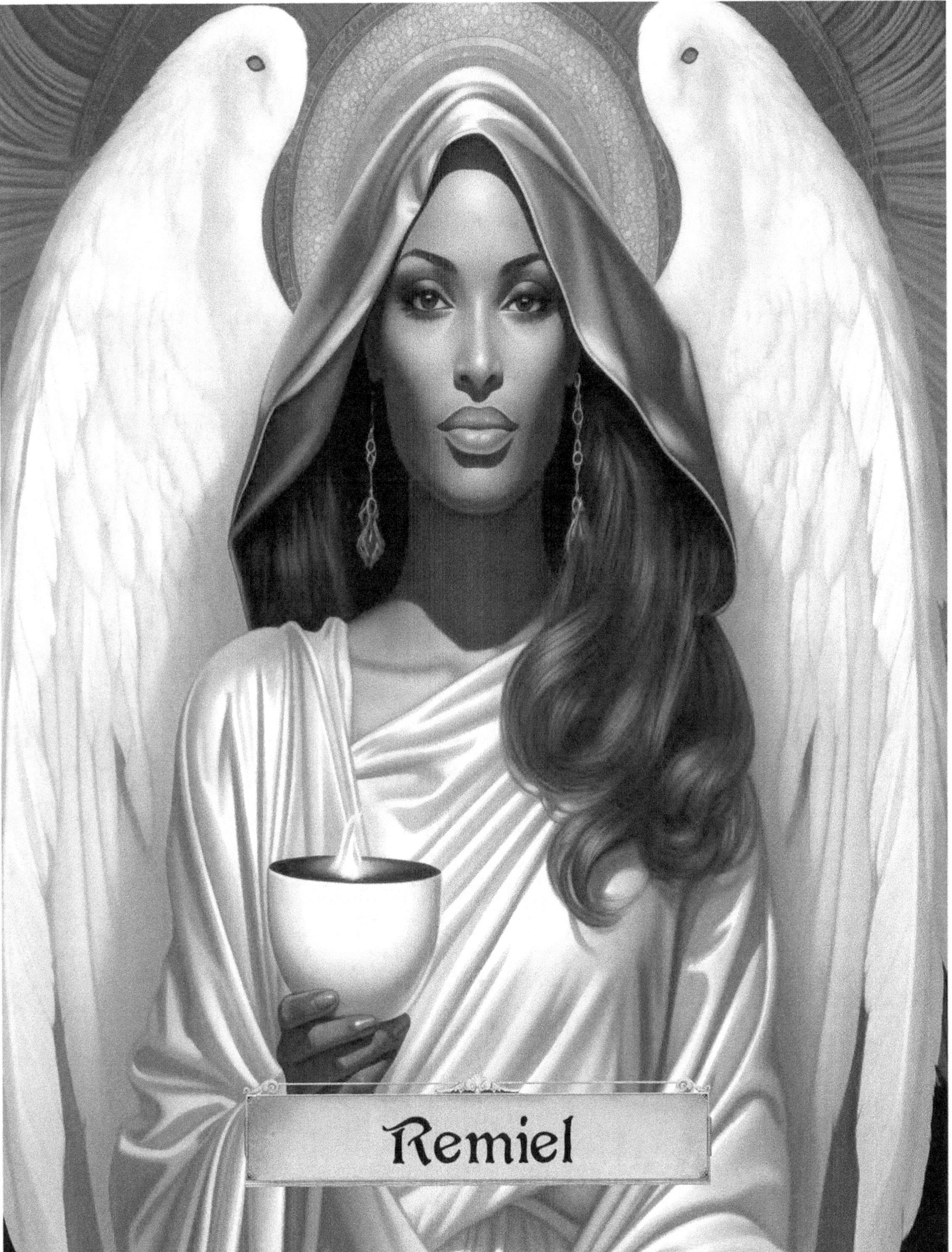
Remiel

Jeremiel,

The angel of prophecy and revelation, embodies insight,
foresight, and the unveiling of destiny.
With his multicolored wings and deep-set eyes,
he guides us towards understanding our purpose
and illuminates the path of our destiny.
Jeremiel helps us interpret dreams and visions,
receive divine guidance, and manifest our highest
potential.

Prayer:

Oh, wise Jeremiel, angel of prophecy and revelation,
I call upon your guidance and insight.
Open my mind to divine messages and
reveal to me my true purpose in life.
Grant me the wisdom to interpret dreams and
visions, and guide me towards fulfilling
my highest potential.
Amen.

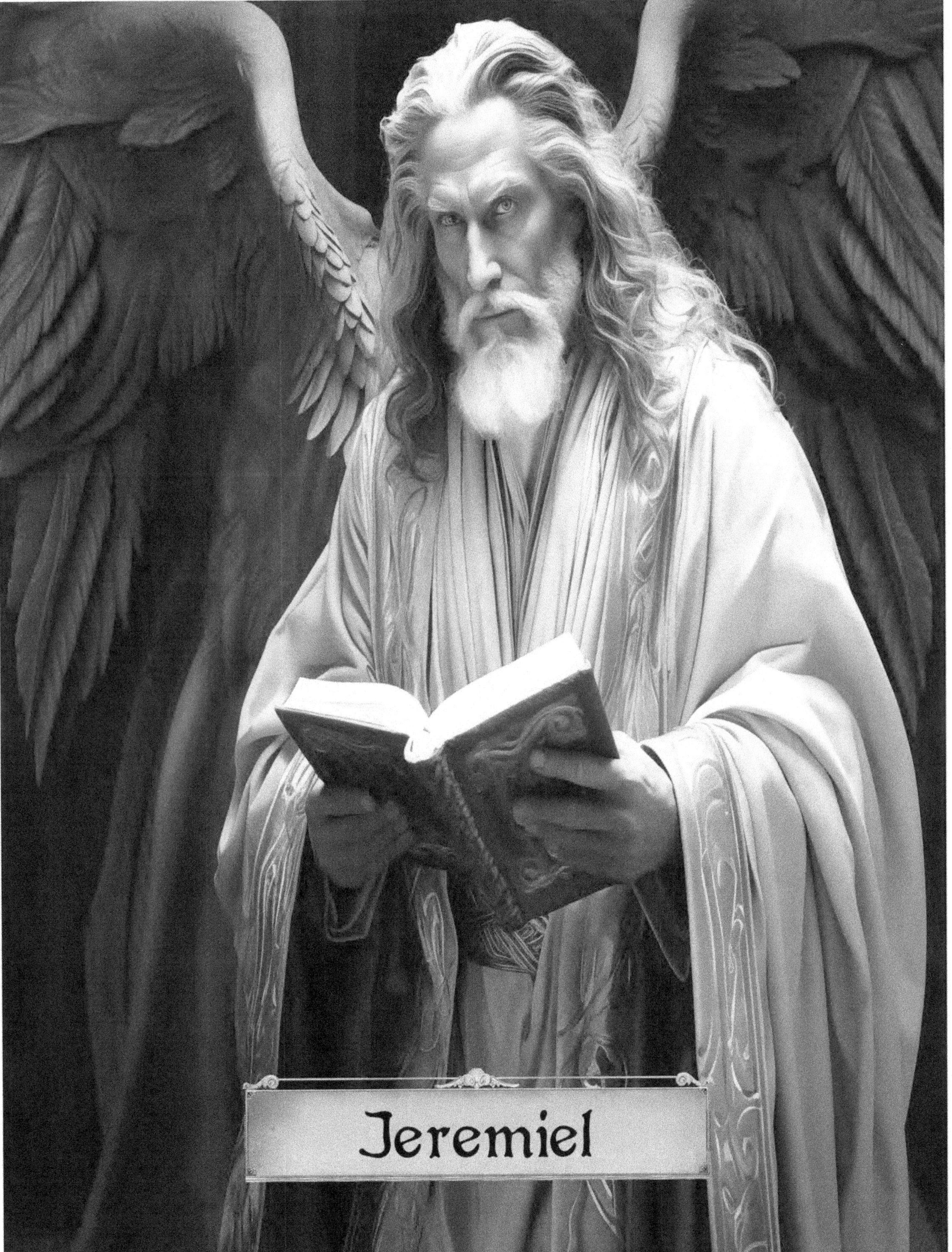
Jeremiel

Keter,

The crown jewel of creation, embodies
the divine essence, pure potentiality, and the source
of all creation. With his ethereal presence and
crown of light, he represents the divine spark
within all beings and the potential for endless growth
and evolution.
Keter guides us towards spiritual awakening,
connection with the divine source, and the manifestation
of our deepest desires.

Prayer:

Oh, radiant Keter, source of all creation
and divine potential, I call upon your infinite
wisdom and grace. Awaken my inner spark
and guide me towards spiritual enlightenment.
Connect me with the divine source within myself
and guide me towards manifesting my
highest aspirations.
Amen.

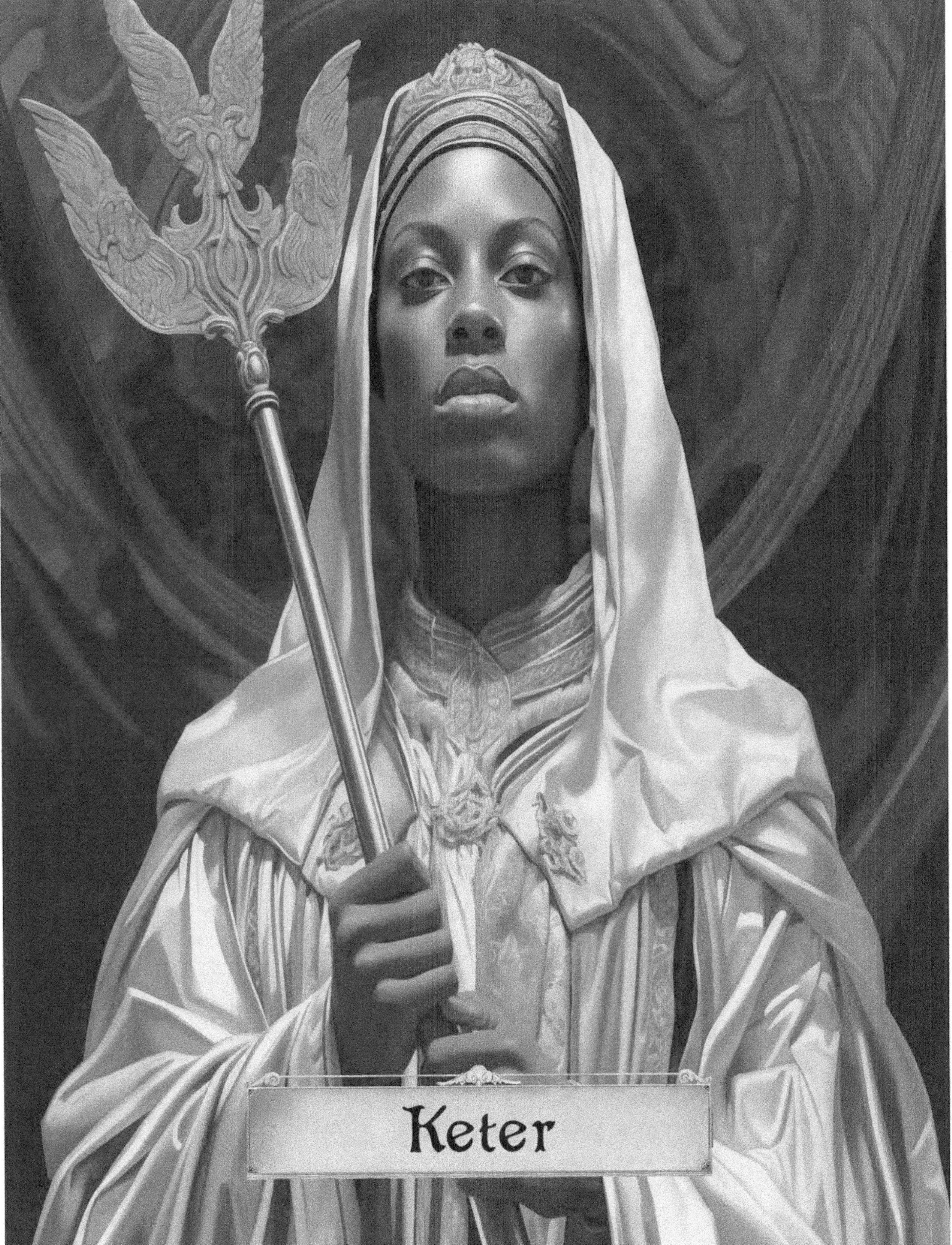
Keter

Da'at,

The angel of knowledge and understanding,
embodies wisdom, discernment, and the ability
to connect seemingly disparate ideas.
With his indigo robes and open book, he represents
the interconnectedness of all knowledge and the
key to unlocking universal understanding.
Da'at guides us towards intellectual growth,
promotes critical thinking, and helps us integrate
different perspectives into a holistic worldview.

Prayer:

Oh, wise Da'at, angel of knowledge
and understanding, I call upon your wisdom and
guidance. Open my mind to new ideas
and perspectives, and help me to discern truth
from illusion. Guide me towards deeper
understanding and wisdom, and enable me
to integrate knowledge into a holistic worldview.
Amen.

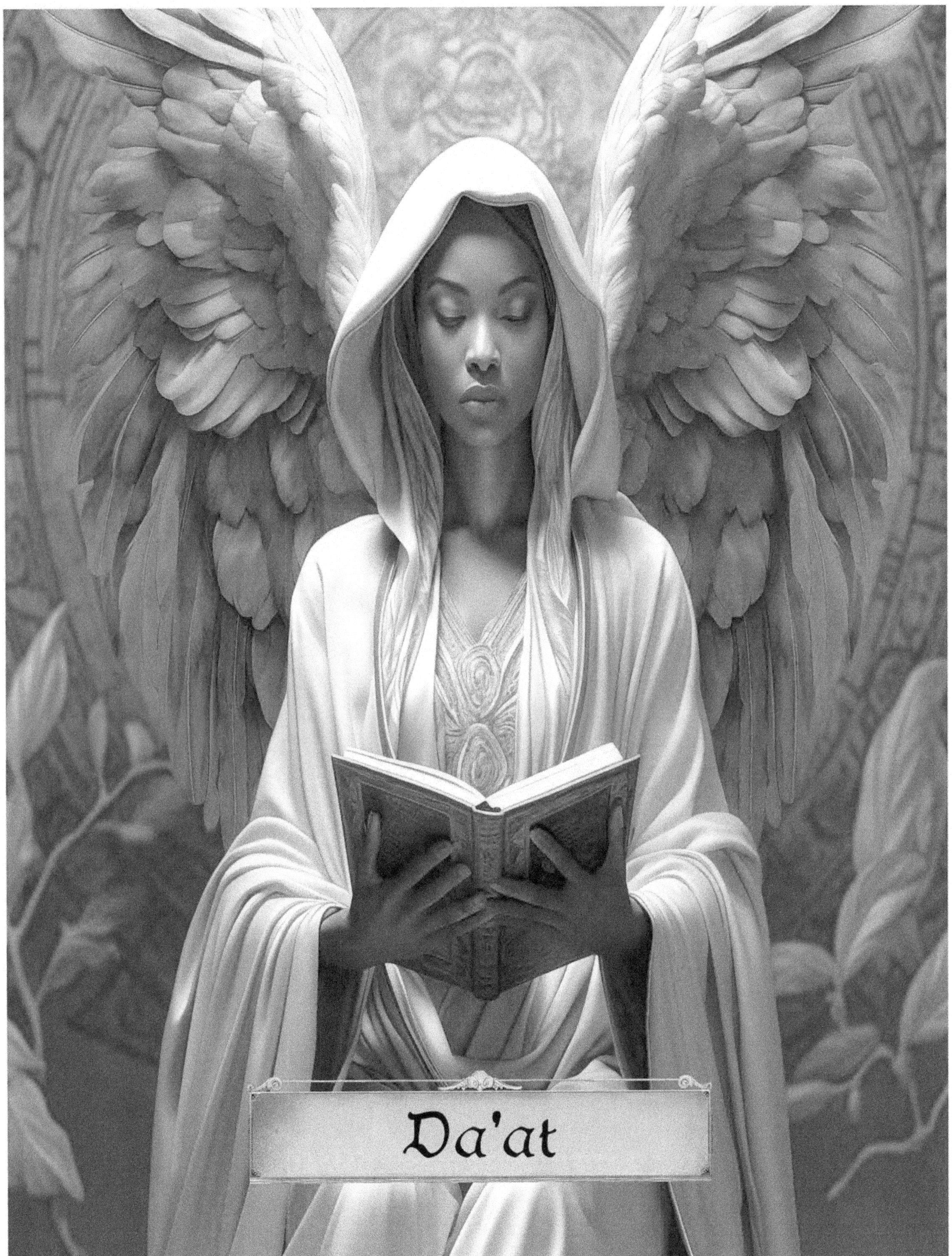
Da'at